Garden Jokes
Jokes About Plants, Flowers, Trees, Fruit and Vegetables

R. J. Clarke

GW00469959

Garden Jokes

What did the bee say to the flower?
Hey bud, what time do you open?

Why is grass dangerous?
Because it has lots of blades

What type of tree has hands?
A palm tree

What tree is always crying?
A weeping willow

What's green and hangs from trees?
Giraffe snot

Why did the gardener plant lightbulbs?
Because she wanted a power plant

Where do gardeners sleep?
In a bed of roses

Why is the Hulk a good gardener?
Because he's got green fingers

Why couldn't the crazy gardener find his allotment?
Because he lost the plot

What is the definition of an acorn?
In a nutshell, it's an Oak tree

Why did the gardener bury his money?
To make his soil rich

Why shouldn't you iron a four leaf clover?
Because you don't want to press your luck

What plant roars?
A dandelion

Why shouldn't you stand near trees?
Because they're shady

What flower does everyone have?
Two-lips

What do trees wear when it floods?
Swimming trunks

What do tree's drink at parties?
Root beer

What did the cactus say to the other cactus?
You're looking sharp

What did trees learn in math class?
Twigonometry

What type of tree loves playing chess?
A chess-nut tree

What is brown and sticky?
A stick

Why was the boy afraid of a plant that had just started shooting?
Because he thought the plant had a gun

What type of tree is not affected by fire?
Ashes because when they are burned they are still ashes

Have you heard about the flower shop being robbed?
It was a violet crime

What type of flower should you give to a saxophone player?
A jazz-min

Where do you plant young children?
Kinder garden

Why did the comedian get booed off for telling bad plant jokes?
Because the jokes were rotten

How does a flower ride a bike?
It petals

What did the soldier say when he heard that the infantry was coming?
At last, we can plant the infant tree

What did the girl say when she dropped her flowers?
Woops-a-daisy

What did the gardener do when he became a manager for a boxer who was losing his fight?
He threw in the trowel

How do you plant a fruit tree?
You berry it

What flower never speaks the truth?
A lilac

How do new gardeners learn?
By trowel and error

Why can't Christmas trees sew?
Because they keep dropping their needles

What did the worm say to the other worm?
Where in the earth have you been?

Which tree has lots of friends?
Poplar tree

What did the plant do to resist being uprooted?
It tried to hold its ground

What do you call a cactus that looks like a cat?
Catcus

How do trees get on to a computer?
They log in

What happened to the plant in math class?
It grew square roots

What month do trees hate?
Sep-timber

What do you call a retired vegetable?
A has-bean

How do you know a spider has been in a cornfield?
There are cob webs

What did the beaver say to the tree?
It's been nice gnawing you

What happens when a plant is sad?
All of the neighboring plants will photo-sympathize with it

What furniture can you make out of flowers?
A flower bed

My wife is leaving me because I have an unhealthy obsession with plants
I said, Where's this stemming from petal

What do you give to a sick citrus tree?
Lemon-aid

What do you get if you cross a monkey with a flower?
A chimp-pansy

Why couldn't the tree find a date?
Because it was too sappy

What do you get if you cross a sheepdog with a flower?
A collie-flower

What did the young flower say to the older flower?
It's not easy living in your shadow

What did the tree do when its bank closed?
It started a new branch

Why do Platanus Occidentalis trees need to see a doctor more than any other tree?
Because they are Sycamore

Why was the cat afraid of the tree?
Because of its bark

What do you get if you divide the circumference of a pumpkin by its diameter?
Pumpkin Pi

How do you get close to a squirrel?
Climb up a tree and act like a nut

Why did the two friends stop spending time together in a treehouse?
They fell out

What did the girl say when a robber stole her fake Christmas tree?
It's not fir

Why did the man struggle tracing his family tree?
Because he wasn't very good at drawing

Why wasn't the dendrochronologist married?
Because the only thing he dated was trees

Why did the idiot hurt himself when he was raking leaves?
He fell out of the tree

What does the letter A have in common with a flower?
They both have bees coming after them

Why couldn't the gardener plant any flowers?
Because he hadn't botany

Why couldn't the tree answer any questions?
Because it was stumped

What game does a cactus play?
Poker

What do you call a scientific tree?
Chemis-tree

What do you call plants that are mad?
Angryculture

What did the apple tree say to the gardener?
Stop picking on me

What do you call a stolen yam?
A hot potato

What did the bee say to the flower?
Hello honey

What is a chicken's favorite vegetable?
Eggplant

What is a pirate's favorite vegetable?
Chaarrrrrd

What is the strongest vegetable?
A muscle sprout

What vegetable would you find in your basement?
A cellar-y

How do you make a strawberry shake?
Put it in the freezer until it shivers

What vegetable is small, round and giggles a lot?
A tickled onion

Why are tomatoes so smart?
Because they are well-read

What do you call a wealthy melon?
A melon-aire

When does someone cut the grass?
When they feel mowtivated

Why did the carrot get embarrassed?
Because it saw the chick pea

What's brown and runs around the garden?
A fence

What is the fastest vegetable?
A runner bean

What do you call a short-tempered gardener?
A snap dragon

Why did the idiot plant Cheerios in his garden?
Because he thought they were donut seeds

What do you call it when worms take over the world?
Global worming

What do you call a nation that only drives pink cars?
A pink carnation

What do you get if you cross some fruit with a necklace?
A food chain

Why did the tomato turn red?
Because it saw the salad dressing

What did the boy say to the plant that was struggling to breathe?
What's the stomata with you

How did the bird say goodbye to the worm?
I'll catch you later

Which herb can't keep a secret?
Only thyme will tell

What does Santa Claus do in his garden?
Hoe, Hoe, Hoe

What did the doctor remove from his salad?
Kidney beans

Why was the cucumber annoyed at the vinegar?
Because it got him in a pickle

What did the grape say when it was trodden on?
It gave a little wine

What fruit do twins eat?
Pears

Why should a banana put sunscreen on?
So that its skin doesn't peel

Why was the strawberry late for work?
Because it was in a jam

How do you make gold soup?
Add 24 carrots

Why are bananas never lonely?
Because they hang around in bunches

How do you make a fruit punch?
Give it some boxing lessons

What did the vegetarian say to the other vegetarian?
Lettuce eat

What do you put on lettuce when it hasn't been dressed?
Cloves

Why do French people eat snails?
Because they don't like fast-food

What do you get if you cross an apple with a crustacean?
A crab apple

Why did the mushroom go to the party?
Because he is a fun guy

What do you get when you cross a canary with a lawnmower?
Shredded Tweet

Why did the man scatter peas all over the world?
Because he wanted peace on Earth

What is a ghost's favorite fruit?
Boo-berry

What do you call a fat pineapple?
A pineapple chunk

What does a cabbage outlaw have?
A price on its head

What do you call corn that joins the army?
Kernel

What's small, green and goes camping?
A Brussel Scout

What is a taxi driver's favorite vegetable?
A cab-bage

What is a kayaker's favorite type of lettuce?
Row-maine

What vegetable do sailors hate?
Leeks

Have you heard the bad joke about the peach?
It's pit-iful

What is a dancer's favorite vegetable?
Spin-ach

What happened when the rhubarb was arrested
He was held in custardy

Why did the people dance to the vegetable band?
Because it had a good beet

What do you call a fast fungus?
A mush-vroom

What is red, small and whispers?
Hoarse radish

What fruit teases people?
A ba...na...na...na...na...na

What vegetable can tie your stomach in knots?
String beans

Where do apples go on vacation?
Fuji

what vegetable likes music?
Beet-root

What did the alien say to the garden?
Take me to your weeder

Why did the idiot plant coins in his garden?
Because he wanted to raise some cash

Why didn't the melons get married ?
Because they cantaloupe

How did the gardener fix his jeans?
With a vegetable patch

What type of fruit can fly?
A goose-berry

What is a scarecrow's favorite fruit?
Straw-berry

When is a pumpkin not a pumpkin?
When you drop it because it then becomes squash

What vegetable has bad manners?
Rude-barb

Why are frogs so happy?
Because they eat what bugs them

What is the coolest vegetable?
Rad-ish

Why did the gardener bring a trowel to his sons bedroom?
Because his wife told him that his son had a weed in his bed

How do corn talk?
With a husky voice

How do succulents greet each other?
Aloe

What type of vegetable can your father make with some scissors?
Pa snips

What is a vampire's favorite fruit?
Neck-tarine

What do you call a gardener that lives dangerously?
Someone living their life on the veg

Why did the raisin go out with a prune?
Because he couldn't find a date

What did the apple skin say to the apple?
I've got you covered

What's orange and sounds like a parrot?
A carrot

Why did the fungus leave the house party?
There wasn't mushroom

Why did the banana go to the doctor?
Because it wasn't peeling very well

Why did the orange cross the road?
To make orange squash

What do you call a banana that likes to dance?
A banana shake

What do you call a depressed berry?
A blueberry

What fruit do trees like the most?
Pine-apple

Have you heard about the garlic diet?
You don't lose any weight but from a distance your friends will think you are thinner

What's the difference between sprouts and boogers?
Kids won't eat sprouts

What type of nuts can hang a picture?
Wall-nuts

What can a whole apple do that half an apple can't?
It can look round

What 's it called when it rains chickens and ducks?
Foul weather

What is worse than finding a worm in your apple?
Finding half a worm

What's green and sings?
Elvis Parsley

Where did the cucumber go for a drink?
In the salad bar

What is the worst vegetable to have on a barbeque grill?
Chard

What type of shoe can you make with a banana skin?
A slipper

What do you get if you cross a potato with an onion?
A potato with watery eyes

If you had 5 apples in your left hand and 7 apples in your right hand. What would you have?
Very big hands

A neighbor popped his head over the fence and asked the gardener, "What are you doing with that manure?" The gardener replied, "I'm putting it on my rhubarb". The neighbor gave a disgusted look and replied, "I usually put custard on mine""

A toddler was in the garden eating a slug. The mother was disgusted by what she saw but curiously asked, "What did it taste like?" The toddler replied, "Worms"

I used to make lots of money clearing leaves from peoples gardens. I was raking it in

Knock knock
Who's there?
Leaf
Leaf who?
Leaf me alone

Knock knock
Who's there?
Lettuce
Lettuce who?
Lettuce in, it's cold outside

Knock. Knock
Who's there?
Apple
Apple who?
Apple on the door but it won't open

Knock. Knock
Who's there?
Figs
Figs who?
Figs your doorbell, it's broken

Knock. Knock
Who's there?
Olive
Olive who?
Olive you with all of my heart

Knock. Knock
Who's there?
Orange
Orange who?
Orange you going to let me in?

Knock. Knock
Who's there?
Pecan
Pecan who?
Pecan someone your own size

Knock. Knock
Who's there?
Turnip
Turnip who?
Turnip the volume, I love this song

Knock. Knock
Who's there?
Avocado
Avocado who?
Avocado cold

Knock knock
Who's there?
Pickle
Pickle who?
Pickle little flower and give it to your mom

33909742R00016

Printed in Poland
by Amazon Fulfillment
Poland Sp. z o.o., Wrocław